KIPOCIHKÂN

Books by Gregory Scofield

The Gathering: Stones For The Medicine Wheel, poetry (Polestar, 1993)
Native Canadiana: Songs from the Urban Rez, poetry (Polestar, 1996)
Love Medicine and One Song, poetry (Polestar, 1997; reprinted by
    Kegedonce Press in 2009)
Thunder Through My Veins, memoir (HarperCollins, 1999)
I Knew Two Metis Women, poetry (Polestar, 1999; reprinted by Gabriel
    Dumont Institute in 2009 with companion CD)
Singing Home the Bones, poetry (Raincoast, 2005)

KIPOCIHKÂN

POEMS NEW & SELECTED

Gregory Scofield

NIGHTWOOD EDITIONS

Nightwood Editions
Box 1779
Gibsons, BC Canada V0N 1V0
www.nightwoodeditions.com

This book has been produced on 100% post-consumer recycled, ancient-forest-free paper, processed chlorine-free and printed with vegetable-based inks.

Cover design: Anna Comfort
Cover photo: Sundance Lodge by Alan and Terri Wagner, www.trekkerphotoart.com
Author photo: Janzen Photography, Winnipeg, Manitoba

Nightwood Editions acknowledges financial support of its publishing program from the Canada Council for the Arts and the Book Publishing Industry Development Program (BPIDP), and from the British Columbia Arts Council.

Canada Council   Conseil des Arts
for the Arts   du Canada

BRITISH COLUMBIA
ARTS COUNCIL
Supported by the Province of British Columbia

Library and Archives Canada Cataloguing in Publication

Scofield, Gregory A., 1966–
    Kipochikân : poems new and selected / Gregory Scofield.

Poems in English and Cree.
ISBN 978-0-88971-228-7

    I. Title.

PS8587.C614 K56 2009   C811'.54   C2009-901371-1

for Michelle, who believed in her Poem-boy;
and for nicîmos, niwicewâkan, Mark

kipocihkân (IPC) A slang word for someone who is unable to talk; a mute.

—*from* Alberta Elders' Cree Dictionary,
Duval House Publishing,
University of Alberta Press, 1998.

CONTENTS

kipocihkân

niya, I am the boy   *me*
whose tongue at birth, kipahikan   *an obstruction*
hungered its blood root
kept sacred by frogs,

the keepers of stories,
âcimowina.   *stories*

niya, I am the one whose mouth,
kipocihkân   *a mute, someone unable to speak*
at night, alone,
is a lodge of words, a frog-song
croaking with sound
I sing from time to time.

êkwa nitwew,   *and I say*
it is a good tongue
housed in a good lodge
that is mostly clean of pity,
of anger.

hâw, êkwa nistam   *but first*
a count of the names
whose tongues
I now call to prayer;

â-haw kisê-manitow   *Oh, Great Spirit*
mâmaw-ôhtawîmaw   *Our Father*

kinanâskomitin   *I give thanks*

nicâpan Mary, my great-great grandmother
whose tongue was made homeless,
shame-shame
the day Riel slipped through the gallows.

pîmatisiwin petamawinân. Amen.   *Bring us life*

â-haw kisê-manitow   *Oh, Great Spirit*
mâmaw-ôhtawîmaw   *Our Father*

kinanâskomitin   *I give thanks*

nicâpanak Johnny êkwa Ida,
my great-grandparents
whose tongues, shame-shame
diluted the gene pool. Whose tongues,
chased up north,
set others to wagging.

pîmatisiwin petamawinân. Amen.   *Bring us life*

â-haw kisê-manitow   *Oh, Great Spirit*
mâmaw-ôhtawîmaw   *Our Father*

kinanâskomitin   *I give thanks*

nimosôm George, my grandfather
whose tongue, at fifty-nine
burst, shame-shame,
an illiterate blood clot. Whose tongue,
down south, he swallowed
for my grandmother.

pîmatisiwin petamawinân. Amen.   *Bring us life*

God, Our Heavenly Father

I give thanks

My grandmother Avis, at ninety-three,
whose tongue, a chorus of etiquette
kept the secret
she hid in the barn
made by her brother. Shame-shame.

Bring us life. Amen.

â-haw kisê-manitow   *Oh, Great Spirit*
mâmaw-ôhtawîmaw   *Our Father*

kinanâskomitin   *I give thanks*

nimâma Dorothy, my mother
whose tongue
swept the halls of psych wards,
her whore days made dead
by pills and wine. Whose tongue,
at forty-eight
she gave back to God. Fuck you!

pîmatisiwin petamawinân. Amen.   *Bring us life*

Ba-ruch A-tah Ado-nai   *Blessed are you, Lord our God,*
E-lo-he-nu Me-lech Ha-olam   *King of the universe*
Toda, Toda.   *I give thanks*

mein papa Ron, my father
whose tongue was a schmatteh   *a rag*
too moth-eaten
to keep all his children.

Alev ha-sholem – from hunger.   *May he rest in peace*
Alev ha-sholem – from harm.
Alev ha-sholem – from pity.
Alev ha-sholem – from shame.
Alev ha-sholem – from our own poisoned tongues.

L'Chaim! Amen.   *To life*

â-haw kisê-manitow   *Oh, Great Spirit*
mâmaw-ôhtawîmaw   *Our Father*
Ba-ruch A-tah Ado-nai   *Blessed are you, Lord our God*
E-lo-he-nu Me-lech Ha-olam   *King of the universe*

Kinanâskomitin   *I give thanks*
Toda, Toda.   *I give thanks*

tapiyaw nîtsânak,   *my half siblings*
mein shvester, mein bruder   *my sister, my brother*
the one before me
whose tongues and names
I pray be sacred in the world,
without shame. Shame.

pîmatasiwin petamawinân.   *Bring us life*
L'Chaim! Amen.   *To life*

God, Our Father

I give thanks

Ann, my stepmother whose tongue,
half charitable, half grudging
held all these years my father's pardon,
my own half tongue
growing back in fragments.
To hell with shame.

Bring us life. Amen.

God, Our Father

I give thanks

Gary, the kimotisk who threw us away,   *thief*
whose tongue, shame-shame
made her heart a morgue, and me,
the one – hope in life – to bury it.

Brings us life. Amen.

God, Our Father

I give thanks

Gerry, the Terrible One whose tongue,
whose fists
left her a pile of broken bones,
shame-shame, and me,
the one – micihciy – to fix her.   *hand*

Bring us life. Amen.

God, Our Father

I give thanks

Sean, the môniyâw-nâpesis whose tongue   *white-boy*
chased me home from school,
his footsteps, shame-shame
reeking of come and awkward hope.

Bring us life. Amen.

God, Our Father

I give thanks

Robert, the Wihtikiw whose tongue,   *Legendary eater of humans*
shame-shame
made marks in my case file,
whose tongue in the dark
made me his boy,
his wild kipocihkân boy.

Bring us life. Amen.
â-haw, kisê-manitow   *Oh, Great Spirit*
mâmaw-ôhtawîmaw   *Our Father*

kinanâskomitin   *I give thanks*

nimâmasis Georgie, my little mother
whose tongue, nehiyawaywin   *the Cree language*
no shame, no shame
I clung to life on.
nehiyawaywin, I clung onto life,

16

her tongue
my kipocihkân hope, my tongue
tasting frog-songs
she brewed in a teapot,
maskihkîwâpoy   *liquid medicine, tea*
she made medicine, her stories
no shame, no shame.

pîmatisiwin petamawinân. Amen.   *Bring us life*

â-haw, kisê-manitow   *Oh, Great Spirit*
mâmaw-ôhtawîmaw   *Our Father*

kinanâskomitin   *I give thanks*

niwicewâkan, the one I go around with
whose tongue, âya, kotak mîna niwî-âtotî, *the one I love*
kâ-kay sakihyak ana ê-wî-acîmak,   *I am going to tell a story about him*
is the rope
I climb back to myself, my lips
the lodge door
he calls me into ceremony, the one
I go around with whose tongue, in the dark,
is a rattle, a frog-song
chasing out kipocihkân.

pîmatisiwin petamawinân. Amen.   *Bring us life*

â-haw, kisê-manitow   *Oh, Great Spirit*
mâmaw-ôhtawîmaw   *Our Father*

kinanâskomitin   *I give thanks*

the ones I've left behind, the ones
whose tongues I've made kipocihkân.

pîmatisiwin petamawinân. Amen.   *Bring us life*

â-haw, kisê-manitow   *Oh, Great Spirit*
mâmaw-ôhtawîmaw   *Our Father*

kinanâskomitin   *I give thanks*

the ones who are my relatives
whose tongues
I've neglected to mention.

pîmatisiwin petamawinân. Amen.   *Bring us life*

piyisk êkwa, I pray   *and last*
the return of frogs,

the keepers of stories,
âcimowina.   *stories*

â-haw, kisê-manitow   *Oh, Great Spirit*
mâmaw-ôhtawîmaw   *Our Father*

kinanâskomitin   *I give thanks*

the ghost
who is my tongue, niyakâtôtamân.   *I am responsible, a plea of guilty*

kinanâskomitin   *I give thanks*

the bitch
who is my tongue, niyakâtôtamân.   *I am responsible, a plea of guilty*

kinanâskomitin   *I give thanks*

the beggar
who is my tongue, niyakâtôtamân.   *I am responsible, a plea of guilty*
kinanâskomitin   *I give thanks*

the glutton
who is my tongue, niyakâtôtamân.   *I am responsible, a plea of guilty*

kinanâskomitin   *I give thanks*

the mute
who is my tongue, niyakâtôtamân.   *I am responsible, a plea of guilty*

kinanâskomitin   *I give thanks*

the singer
who is my tongue, niyakâtôtamân.   *I am responsible, a plea of guilty*

pîmatisiwin nipetamawîna. hâw!   *Bring me life. Amen*

(2009)

THE GATHERING

Stones for the Medicine Wheel

Call Me Brother

"You never know when you're talking to an Indian," he
says wisely because I am only half which we both know
is not the real issue but the way I look which makes it
next to impossible not to spot me sticking out at a
powwow because I have the tourist look that offends
my darker relations who don't see me as related but a
wannabe muzzling up around the drum to sing 49ers
except I feel the beat like my own heart racing when
curious eyes study if I am just mouthing the words or
actually belting them out because I am a true diehard
Skin with blue eyes that really screws up the whole
history book image except my roots can't be traced to
the Bering Strait but nine months after European
contact which to this day hasn't been forgiven even
though we all have some distant grandpa who at one time
or another took an Indian wife which we tend to forget
because anything but pure is less than perfect and we
all secretly need someone to be better than so the
next time you see me up dancing call me brother

Different Loads

Here on the West Coast we got our own place.
Claiming a park downtown is simple—pass out on a
Bench. No hang-ups when it comes to stringing our
Rags in public. Hang-out darks with whites. You either
Come from the same hamper or you don't.

Uptown whites are an entirely different load. They
Get stained behind closed doors, at cocktail parties
Or business luncheons. Moving along their corporate
Clothesline you got to have a certain satin appeal—
Burlap wear. One day you get the permanent press
Treatment—the next you're bounced.

Indians got the right idea. An old wringer washer does
One hell of a good job. Who needs a dry cleaner to
Keep secrets? We share ours come washing day.

One Tough Skin Sister

Her face looks like it's been through a meat grinder.
Coming off a wine drunk, it looks even worse. She
should be six feet under, at least one foot buried

but some unseen power gave her nine lives. Probably
a goddamned man too, she adds. I don't blame her.
Her mouth is still pretty swollen: purple-red lips
without expression

though when going on about finally getting electricity
up north, she squeezes out a joke—how pissing in
the dark you needed a seeing-eye dog.

Getting a one-way to the coast was a smart move.
The only drawback, her grandkids. Hard to imagine
her being a granny, howling her warsong through chipped
teeth, telling how all those smart-assed brothers
wore out their sorry welcome.

Just Medicine

Someone got even on that old bugger
held up on crutches
making his way into town
dragging his bum leg behind
those support boots look so heavy
swollen-up feet cursing inside
not the same gutter language
I remember going over my head
but I knew F meant something nasty
he got his sleazy thrills
liking the feel of each dirty word
my mom did her shopping quickly

Paying half down on a bottle
she was good for it so no problem
except the usual free sample
only one because I tagged along
making sure she came home
I was her little watchdog
ready to attack if he got too cheeky
he just sat there minding his p's & q's
though, in his later years
he must have gotten greedy for a touch
running up against some powerful shawoman
into bad medicine

Divided

My beigey-pink shade
Unlike you with bronze skin
I'm a Skin without colour; I get the brush-off
Ego-tripping on me again
Deciding if I am pure enough   Red enough
To be whole but the whole of me says
Enough of this colour crap
I am not your white whipping-boy

Growing up in an all-white town
I never forgot my red half   It counted big
Especially if you looked not right white
But wrong white   To white people that's off-white
Dirty white in Sally Ann clothes
You got followed in stores
They just asked a lot if you needed help   Not help
To find the right size but to the door   To the cop shop
If you got caught stealing
That was it   no second chance
They just nailed your raggedy ass to the wall
Never mind in school
You kept your head down   Ducked the put-downs
Shoved it all down

What a Way to Go

Middle of the month
We're so hard pressed
Hunting through every pocket

Hoping I stashed
A little something away
Teasing gum wrappers show up

My lucky prize jingling
Deep down between the lining
Escaped coins just frustrate

What is her majesty
Doing for supper tonight?
Fry bread sounds good

We might have moose
If we were bush Indians
But our appetite is city cuisine

Back home our elders
Have ancient taste buds
Wintertime they stock up

Long-distance hunting stories
Confirm who is a good grandson
Staying put keeping freezers filled

Coming together to feast
It all seems so simple
Taking from the land, being thankful

In the city we hunt each other
Looking to borrow some flour, sugar, tea
Just enough to get by till the end of the month

Taste of Hatred

I was too young
hearing that word Aryan
my first taste of hatred I
groaned my way through
Alex Haley's *Roots*

cross burnings & "Amazing Grace"
left me cringing
I had to ask my mom
what is a nigger?
White people's fear, she said
we all bleed red blood

but who could believe that after
reading about the Holocaust
even those ghastly pictures
were no guarantee
that fascist purity wouldn't
soil every generation

back then, how easy for me
hating every pale face
I was all Indian
listening to Buffy Sainte-Marie
chanting my history
downtown

the worst I saw
in Vancouver up close
one of my own
slugging his wife for booze money
her broken look
filled my mouth with bile

Nothing Sacred

Excavate: uproot a granny
                                   gets a new resting place   pay
                                   five bucks to view her in a
                                   Plexiglas tomb

New Age Movement: b & e our healing lodge
                                   making off with our medicine
                                   bird   so much for your
                                   exhausted Buddha on the altar

Fashion: Pocahontas makes *Vogue* in
                                   that two-piece buckskin
                                   trim your fantasy with fringe
                                   and beads   feathers tacky

Tourist Traps: only place to get a genuine
                                   Wong & Sons totem pole
                                   deciphering clan designs
                                   extra

Read All About It: Pigeon Park Indians make
                                   Premier an honorary drinking
                                   chum   big powwow
                                   scheduled after party

For Now: steal our spotlight   his high
                                   profile   mixing promises
                                   and Lysol

Private Thoughts on a Warm Night

Your body is cool, sensual, perfect to the touch
this wilting heat wave makes it impossible to sleep
just lay there thinking back to earlier tonight
your thirsting eyes drank me in,
what we could do if I'd invited you
up for tea, some slow-moving music
we're not sure   have to play it by ear
maybe just smile a lot, pretend we don't sneak peeks
but we know better it's a matter of timing
silence   private thoughts are worth more unspoken
even when the mind races ahead
doesn't know where to begin   I start with the top
button   work my way down slowly   letting it just
happen   don't go too quickly   save it & have some
special feeling to remember   like waves drenching my
body   while the moon swells to twice its normal size

NATIVE CANADIANA

Songs from the Urban Rez

Nikâwî

The world began
through the V of her legs,
a wishbone expanding
that never broke.

My right foot
lodged between her ribcage
was only a hint
of the pain to come.

Thirteen hours it took
before she could breathe
Paskowi-pîsim   *July or the Moulting Moon*
into my mouth and smile.

. . .

Twenty-nine summers
the Moulting Moon eclipsed
his ghost
never once disturbed my dreams
not even when the phone rang and rang
that's how missed he was.

ochichisa / her hands

they were the same hands
that changed diapers /
gave whippings /
held and spoke volumes /
all throughout
the turbulent years /
and finally the silent hours /
when I pleaded
for even a disjointed memory /
something tangible
to hold onto like green /
her favourite colour
even the sickly green
of soiled bedsheets
or curtains
that wisp shut
in one motion /
I could tolerate / even stand
if it weren't for her
pushing mine away
or squeezing them
with the knowledge
of her leaving /
that I refused to accept
because they were
still so strong
from my hanging on /
and the diligent vigil
I kept / praying
for the lush green
of spring / or an end
to the orphaned winter /
until there was nothing

to pray for / hope for /
hold onto / for the last time
I held those same hands
that changed diapers /
gave whippings /
held and spoke volumes /
all in such a short
short time

Wrong Image

Yeah, their necks were stiff
from watching Indians downtown
who'd piss in the back alley
closing time.
From their cars
they were safe, those honkies.
We knew they were there
skulking around
like a weak species
trying to build themselves up.

In high school
Emma and me
were the only Indians.
We started hanging out together
formed the very first
least likely to succeed club.
None of those white kids
could down a mickey
of rye like us.
We didn't even need a mixer—
just pop off the cap
and chug-a-lug.

Sometimes they'd stand
out on the street
straining to hear our drunk talk.
We spoked pretty broken
so when dey mimicked our dalk
it was authentic not Hollywood.

They joked about our appearance
said we picked
leftovers at Sally Ann.
Once at recess
we overheard them laughing
and gave each one
a damn good wallop.

In the school library
where I thought and brooded
a long time
I crouched over history books
staring sullen
at those stoical faces.
Me and Emma
got names too.
I was her chief
and she my squaw—
only she humped anything
I was too stupid to notice.

Last summer
I spent the afternoon with a journalist.
I wore linen and leather sandals,
spoke of racism and class
and why I began writing.
The interview was about survival
and healing.
In the article
I read he was disturbed
by the predominance of alcohol

in my work—
how I perpetuated
the negative image of native people.

Walking the beach later
so many white skins
sprawled and craving
earth colouring, a cool beer
I smiled stupid and wondered
whatever became of Emma.

Cycle (of the black lizard)

It was a priest
who made him act that way
so shy he wouldn't say shit if
his mouth was full of it.
At least that's what his
old lady said
each time her face got smashed
with his drunk fist.
The last time
he just pushed her around
then passed out. Later,
her kôhkum said   *grandmother*
a lizard crawled inside his mouth
and laid eggs.

It was a black lizard, she said
the kind who eat the insides
feasting slowly
until their young are hatched.
Already his tongue was gone
from so much confessing.
Other boys at the boarding school
never talked out loud
for fear the lizard
would creep into their beds.
At first it just moved around
inside his head
manoeuvring serpentine
like a bad dream.

Then one night
his brain caved in & oozed out
his ears, nose and mouth.

It was his mouth
that caused so much trouble.
In there was rotten teeth
and stink breath
made by that gluttonous lizard.
Morning Mass
he swallowed hard to rid the slime
but night-time it just returned
and slithered around.

Another boy, only older
had the same trouble.
Recess
they eyed each other's dirty holes
and spit, spit, spit.
Once they got caught
and had to scrub the stairs—
and neither said shit about it.

At school, the teacher
noticed his kids had dull eyes
and never spoke or laughed.
The girl was ten
and developed for her age.
When asked in class to tell an Indian story
she went crimson in her face
and cried.
Every few days
her brother got sent
to the principal's office.
They thought he was just naturally rough,
like all Indians.

What they didn't know
was in her pee-hole, his mouth
a lizard crawled around
leaving eggs
during the Lord's prayer.

Stepfather

He stole the sun,
spoke thunder
coming down the mountain
only too proud
to swallow the last rays.

Like raven
he kept any warmth
sealed tight
in a box.
Never ask or beg
she said, her eyes
loose hinges
on a swinging door.

I knew then
not all storms
were good.

Promises

not always did I have an aversion
to shiny objects, convenient arrangements

beneath the buffalo robe

snuggle into him   temporary
the famine his doeskin fingers snail
across my lips of strawberry pleasure

beneath the buffalo robe

spread my arms, my legs
I offer moose tongue and berries
generations he devours in seconds

beneath the buffalo robe

I don't get sweet-talked easy
his hands know what to do
in the dark / light of day

beneath the buffalo robe

promises he whispers   temporary
the taste his foreign tongue snakes
through ravines, over valleys

beneath the buffalo robe

each kiss
history
lolls on the tip of my tongue

Piss 'n' Groan

When the sun comes out
the streets smell like piss
down here
it doesn't matter what side
of the skids
you're on
you could be better than me
I really don't give a damn
if you think so
why not just say so
I won't crumble
because you got a swollen-up head

That lump could be
from a wagon burner like me
who wouldn't play the dirty Indian
just off the rez role
because you got an inferiority complex
being one of the few
under-classy winos
who can't afford to be
a white alcoholic   unlike me
I got so much lower-class
I far surpass
their usual upper-class groan

How they got to pay taxes
and we don't
as if we said 500 years ago
put that in the treaty
while you're at it
roll out that whiskey keg
and don't forget to include

an educational clause
if we're going to be force-fed
your glamorous take-over history
why not get paid to act
the conquered part   the part where we say
hey, môniyâs I want my cheque   *non-native person*
gimme my cheque right now
you owe me
for this leftover land
we never sold, gave up, handed over

Don't tell me
we got no rights here
just because you got the Legislation
to steal and expropriate
without our consent
that doesn't mean
there was no law here
before you stuck your big toe
across the line   tap danced all over
the continent like it was yours
to begin with
why all this pissing and groaning
whether we got the inherent right
to stop you from dumping
your pesticides or polluting the planet

Who needs all that colonial crap anyway
saying I'm just another
loudmouth Indian
rattling off anti-white propaganda
is justification that any cohesive
future together is pissed away already

because you don't want to hear
all my pissing 'n' groaning
even if I suggested
we piss 'n' groan collectively
that still wouldn't heal
the damage done
maybe even now
I've groaned more harm than good
but who gives a damn
my groaning job is throwing it all back
to look at
whoever wants to get pissy
go right ahead
I'm not gonna cry about it

Tough Times on Moccasin Blvd

Battered rez dog look
Sulking down up back again
Zigzag the usual dopers ducking

Behind the hotel dumpster
Divers do it for free
These addicts sit defeated corpses

Crouched on their hunchback bone
Bent and twisted hovering over
A singular dirty rig

Pricks transparent skin holding together
A framework of jelly bones inside
Shooting galleries they sprawl

On a beat-up mattress tripping
On their rez dog tongues wagging
And drool and bob their shrunken heads

Up down up down and
Down the street they zigzag
Flock starved like pigeons and

Hover around the needle van
Shrieking obscure dialect and shriek
Their rez dog mumbo-jumbo

Earsplitting as a mausoleum
scattering the shouts of death
Up down and back again

Mixed Breed Act

How do I act   I act without an Indian act
Fact is I'm so exact about the facts
I act up when I get told I don't count
Because my act's not written

So I don't get told who I am or where to go
If I want to hang solo without my tribe
Check out other rezless Indians
No DIA director can pop me on a bus

Send me home   homeless as I am
I'm exact about my rights
So exact in fact I act downright radical
Though never hostile unless provoked

To extract the truth
Truth is my treaty number's not listed
So I don't get obscene phone calls
From politicians breathing heavy in my ear

Or dirty Bill C31 talk
Still I'm authentic enough to be counted
A genuine artifact not so much pre-Columbian
But darn close

So I mark my X for self-government
And wait to be noticed
Not me alone as extinct
But distinct as we are

Once we were good enough
To be aboriginal even original Canadians

Way back before they took up hockey
And claimed our lakes

Those immigrants were too busy
Playing hookey on our grandmothers
To notice they left behind a new nation
To run their stolen country

Colonized as it was
It was already occupied and never sold
Why defend our claim
Both sides end up taking all the credit

So we end up scrunched in between
Suffocating ourselves to act accordingly
However we're told to act
But according to their act

I'm not solely a First Nations act
Or Canadian act
But a mixed breed act
Acting out for equality

This is not some rebel halfbreed act
I just scribbled down for revenge
Besides
I don't need to be hung

For my mixed mouth blabbing
How they used their act
To cover up
Dirty goings-on in our country

Not Too Polite Poetics

his diagnosis was not conclusively cutting edge
nor was the conversation charming
like was I a closet peace-pipe smoker
or did I eat rabbits
with the fur still on

but what was my teepee creeping technique
did I make my move closing time
sneak up cruise past
make those
heads tilt eyes swing
just this way, boy

or simply hang around,
looking seductively stoic
like a Curtis portrait
waiting and contemplating
their move

out west I discovered
I didn't need to kiss up
to graduate head of the class
despite the prerequisite
keeping my mouth in check

not polite to stick my grudge nose
in their Native Lit class
say my piece on First Nations first voice
demand Kinsella visit Hobbema
or take a course in Cree colloquial syntax

like all First Nations writers
I must adhere to ethnic demands
make my poet's entrance
wrapped in a Pendelton blanket
sunburst geometric design

maybe a Navajo ring or two
to give me the authentic look
a ghost dance shirt
might come in handy
reflecting history bullets

when I get too mouthy
for their comfort
they want Yeats Dickinson Longfellow
a cozy chit-chat afterward

I barely pass the visiting poet's test,
answer why I'm so angry
so impolite, so defensive
is not what I want here
but the chance to speak

without backs up or a drum solo

The Poet Leaves a Parting Thought

hâw, ni-nêhiyawêyân and   *now, I speak Cree*
their English tags behind my every word
word is my rez city lingo
is good enough to get
a bona fide *hmm* from the white audience
maybe even a raised eyebrow
if I really wow 'em
with my dangling modifier talk
in my own Indigenous way
I can be pretty preverbed   *in between a verb and perverted*
when I want

appropriate recognition
I get the usual inconclusive oh
although my buffalo robe talk
can be darn sexy
when I flavour it up with some Cree spice
why waste my breath
on Columbus hot talk
I just end up making him into
a Don Juan hero
as if his slaver descendants
deserve that fame

but it could happen
if I don't give my tongue
a native language mammogram
check it regularly
for English lumps and bumps
I run the chance of becoming
totally anglicized

I wouldn't understand if an elder said
âtayohikî, boy   *to tell a legend or myth*

I'd have to go back to school
for proper instruction

then I'd be just another wannabe book-talker
not an Indigenous oral talker like I am
but a multicultural professor
talker / bragger
bragging how I know up-shot Indians
but what's there to brag about bragging
I don't make $70,000 a year
doing anthropological digs in Peru
more like AIDS studies
because I see these corpses daily
dragging themselves around the city

looking for food or shelter
they just keep popping up
new off the rez
need a place to stay
nowhere to go except Catholic Charities
a transition house
if you're really black 'n' blue
maybe detox
if you've been on an extended bender
I make the appropriate referral
go home scream and write

create dark talk
for white talkers to talk about

I might not be the best
Indigenous poet but hey, my English is lousy enough
to be honest

LOVE MEDICINE AND ONE SONG

Ceremonies

I heat the stones
between your legs,
my mouth,
the lodge where you come
to sweat.

I fast your lips
commune with spirits,
fly over berry bushes
hungering.

I dance with sun,
float with clouds
your earth smell
deep in my nostrils,
wetting
the tip of my tongue.

I chant with frogs,
sing you to dreams,
bathe you in muskeg,
wrap you in juniper
and sweet-pine.

nîcimos, for you   *sweetheart or lover*
I drink blessed water,

chew the bitter roots
so the medicine is sweet,
the love, sacred.

My Drum, His Hands

over the bones, over the bones
stretched taut
my skin, the drum

softly he pounds
humming

as black birds dance,
their feathers
gliding over lips, they drink
the stars
from my eyes
depart like sun
making way for moon
to sing, to sing
my sleeping

my sleeping song
the sky bundle

he carries me to dreams,
his hands wet
and gleaming

my drum aching

His Flute, My Ears

piyis êkwa ê-tipiskâk êkwa   *At last it was night*
ôh, êkwa kâ-kimiwahk,   *oh, and it rained,*
kâ-kimiwahk   *it rained*

earth smells, love medicine
seeping into my bones
and I knew
his wind voice
catching
the sleeping leaves

ôh, êkwa kâ-kimiwahk,   *oh, and it rained,*
kâ-kimiwahk   *it rained*

I dreamed
him weaving spider threads
into my hair,
fingers of firefly
buzzing ears, the song
his flute
stealing clouds from my eyes

kâ-kimiwahk   *it rained*
I woke

numb in my bones.

Offering: 1996

This long drought
scorches the skin,
blisters me in places

most vulnerable; inner thighs,
tailbone, nape of neck
the sacred temples.

Since your body eclipsed
I've swallowed the moon,
pretended light from others

and my bones did crack
and from my mouth
grew many unhappy weeds.

Where once were drums
and flutes and songs
there is silence,

incurable as the heart, hopeless
like your resurrection
I breathe all my breath

to conjure
what I hold most sacred:

your full, coaxing mouth,
the two perfect moles
I've named and kissed
the back of your legs,

that smooth dip
between your cheeks, the musk
from the shell of your arms

which left underwater
is a potion, a drug
lulling me to dizziness,

lifting me upward
like sage and cedar
singing to the heavens, singing

to guide you home.

ohpahôwi-pîsim

august • the flying-up moon

Most unexpected,

you roll into me like a stone
sinking deep in the earth,
settling deeper
than all the moons
having crawled across the sky,
crouched low and silent,
soft-boned and remorseful
as the skinny willows
rattling in the wind.

Now
I cannot name your absence
or its taste,
a strange language
neither bitter nor sweet.

Only you've returned,
a heavy-winged bird
and the bed is a pulse
with the weight of desire,
songs that swim beneath our skin,
lay drunk like fish
in stifling n pools.

Though this longing is no secret
you hold it close,
press into me, helpless
against your shame.

Finally you've come!
piko kîkway miyonâkwan.   *everything is beautiful*

You sing the summer's end
between my thighs, kiss
the swollen moon
in the curve of my belly,

me, flying up
like the ducks in the marsh,
you, new-feathered,
and weightless,

ushering the dancers to my lips.

More Rainberries (The Hand Game)

The softest, deepest warmth
between his shoulders
is where my lips
take momentary rest, where
breathing becomes ritual
transcends into ceremony

pushing the song up and out
of his skin
so lowly he sings
rainberries form and glisten,
finding my tongue

each mole, every fine hair
speaking the soul's language,
tossing up
the body's ancient rhythm
like hand game bones,
painted sticks marking
the secret centres, where

my hands, delirious with song
sway to his drumming,
rock to each beat swooping
down, down
to the muskeg, where

scented rainberries
fat as frogs
explode in my mouth,

his deepest warmth

a sweet taste
painting my lips.

Earth and Textures
for Kim

îh, îh   *Look, look*
she is the earth lodge
opening her arms,
softly calling,
pî-pîhtâkwey, pî-pîhtâkwey.   *come in, come in*

îh, îh   *Look, look*
she is pîhtwawikamik   *the sacred lodge where the pipe is smoked*
where I come
to cry the dry stone
from my throat.

îh, îh   *Look, look*
she is earth medicine ties
hanging from trees,
a sacred moon mother
birthing stars
for my dream path.

pehtâw, pehtâw   *Listen, listen (as in to hear very closely)*
she is the song
of frogs and crickets
tickling my feet
so always I am rooted.

I KNEW TWO METIS WOMEN

Dah Ting About Waltzing

is, she said,

never let dah wooman leet

cause if you do

she'll dake yer pants,

make you sign yer cheques

an hant dem over,

push you outta bet

to feet dah babies,

do dah dishes, if she wishes

make you hem her slacks,

go an get flour from dah store

to bake hers a gake,

ice dah damn ting, too.

Best ting, she said,

are dah ones

who step on yer does.

Heart Food

for Marilyn Dumont

Pine-Sol is the smell of home
where handmade curtains
trimmed with lace
warmed winter windows, where

baking bread, loaves fat and soft
as pillows,
hung under my nose, woke
my taste buds

to stewing moose meat
and whipped potatoes,
kissed my lips
with sweet apple or cherry pie,

where mugs of hot tea
heaped with sugar, evaporated milk,
were later slurped at the table strewn
with glass beads,

flower templates and moccasin tongues,
scraps of smoked moose hide
tanned out back of Caroline's place
and sent from Alberta

with old slacks, sweaters
and blouses
that no longer fit, that hemmed
and altered became like new,

new like the second-hand dolls
she washed and dressed
in miniature petticoats, perfectly stitched
dresses and boots

who jigged on the shelf
to fiddle tunes, whose tiny hands
clapped along to records
or conducted

her guitar songs
long after I fell to sleep,
the smell of Pine-Sol,
smoked moose hide, cinnamoned apples

etching their way
silently into my knowing,
running deeper than the blood
feeding my heart.

Going to Get Uncle

The cops showed up that time
escorting Uncle
and his damn good shiner
to pack some things.

"Shh, kiya keepeekiskweet,"   *Shh, don't say anything*
she whispered,
shaking her head
like an old time chief
so as not to sign the treaty
or give away
the last buffalo,
unlike Uncle
who hummed and hawed,
skittered about,
grabbing the clock,
dirty tea towels and socks.

"Wa, puksees!" she rasped   *Oh God, the mouse!*
when no one was looking,
an invisible thread
sewing her lips
into a smirk.

After,
I asked how he got
the puffed eye.

"He falled on dab goffee dable,"
she said, stacking the empties
back in their case.

"Hmm . . . must have had help,"
I said, a little elder
chewing my top lip.

Her laughter shattered the silence
like the beer bottle in the sink.

"Well," she confessed,
"dat ole bugger hat it comin.
Wants to run aroun
night an day. So boom!
I let heem have it
right on hees fat face"

"Ann-tee!" I protested,
"No wonder he brought the cops."

"Ah, never mind," she said,
waving her hand.
"To hell wit heem."

But by noon
we sat on her bed
in front of the mirror
and the transformation began.

Sober as a judge,
she brushed the knots
from her hair,
rolling it into a bun.
The paint—"her warpaint,"
she called it—
brought her lips and cheeks

back to life.
And finally,
a few quick Avon sprays
to appease the gods.

Rummaging through the fridge
a sandwich was made
from leftovers,
sliced cheese and pickles
and one stray
blueberry bannock.

"Blue bannock for dah blue eye,"
she chuckled, heading out the door.
"Dah ole bugger will like dat."

Oh, Dat Agnes

Wuk-wa, Aunty would roar
between chipped teeth
and slap her leg
so the dogs jumped and barked.

You know, she told me,
Her fadder was a Swede, uh.
But boy, coult she ever
speak goot Cree.

One dime
we hat to glean dah ghapel
an I says to her,
"Hey Agnes, I wonder
what dah fadder's always drinkin?"

"I dunno," she says,
shruckin hers shoulders like dis.

"Well, it must be goot," I says,
"cause bees always drinkin it.
Maybe we shoult try some, uh?"

"Oh my, Georgie," she says
makin a fat kokoos face.   *pig*
"Mmm . . . dis is goot."

"Wa, mucheementow!" I says to her   *Oh my, devil!*
an crabbed dat chug o' wine.

Well dah next ting you know
we forget all about dah ghapel.

Den dat grazy ting started singin.
Boy oh boy,
shes sounded like a coddamn gat
howlin at dah moon.

Well, we finished off dat chug
an started on dah next one.

"Hey, what about dis song?" I says.

"I ton't gare what dey say
all dah mooneeyas iskwaysuk   *all the white girls*
keetasay . . ."   *pull down their pants*

Well, dat Agnes
was laughin so hart
she farted an falled over.

Holy gripe, next ting you know
dat Sister Tennis
game chargin up to dah alter
an says,
"Hey, you geerls!
What's going on in here!"

An dat was dat.
Boy, did we ever gatch hell.
Hers dad laughed about it, dough,
toll everyone
we got trunk on Ghrist's blood.

Wuk-wa, mucheementowak! She'd chuckle   *Oh my goodness, devils!*
lighting another cigarette.

An dere was dah dime we . . .

Not All Halfbreed Mothers
for Mom, Maria

Not all halfbreed mothers

drink

Red Rose, Blue Ribbon,
Kelowna Red, Labatt's Blue.

Not all halfbreed mothers
wear cowboy shirts or hats,
flowers behind their ears
or moccasins
sent from up north.

Not all halfbreed mothers
crave wild meat,
settle for hand-fed rabbits
from Superstore.

Not all halfbreed mothers
pine over lost loves,
express their heartache
with guitars, juice harps,
old records shoved
into the wrong dustcover.

Not all halfbreed mothers
read *The Star, The Enquirer,
The Tibetan Book of the Dead*
or Edgar Cayce,
know the Lady of Shalott
like she was a best friend
or sister.

Not all halfbreed mothers
speak like a dictionary
or Cree hymn book,
tell stories
about faithful dogs
or bears
that hung around or sniffed
in the wrong place.

Not all halfbreed mothers
know how to saddle
and ride a horse,
how to hotwire a car
or siphon gas.

Not all halfbreed mothers

drink

Red Rose, Blue Ribbon,
Kelowna Red, Labatt's Blue.

Mine just happened
to like it

Old Style.

She's Lived

ten lives, ten beat-up lives,
ten thousand years

in the Safeway parking lot,
feeding her dogs
from the dumpster,

holed-up
in her station wagon,
no place to go.

She's lived
in old meat trucks,
converted them into home,
tacked up pictures
scattered rag rugs and treasures
so you could smell
her old memories.

She's lived
in town, rented shacks
from the municipality,
from white landlords
who never fixed the heat
or the stove that leaked gas
and gave her headaches

ten thousand years.

She's lived

day to day,
hocked her guitar

to pay the hydro, buy tobacco,
a few cold beers
to wash down
all the things
she wasn't supposed to say,
bitch or complain about
when she got evicted
because someone's mother or daughter
needed a place
or the rent got jacked up

jacked up so high
she'd leave, take her dogs
back to the parking lot,
eating cold beans
by the interior light,

reading by flashlight
about stars who got facelifts
or landed cozy deals
or what her horoscope said,
though it never came true.

The truth was

she lived

ten lives, ten thousand years,

prehistoric
and yet to be discovered.

One day
her forty-eight-year-old bones
simply gave up

and no one batted an eye.

They Taught Her

for Louise, Sky-Dancer

praying, bruised on the knees,
was the right way,
that God, an old whiteman,
only heard
Hail Marys, Our Fathers.

They taught her

how to make beds,
thick bread and whipped potatoes,
where to put the plates,
knives and forks,

where the pleats go
in Father's slacks, his robe
for Mass,
where the candles are set,
the chalice and bell,
what to polish them with.

They taught her

French was civilized
and even holy things in Cree
didn't compare,
that nicknames for the Sisters
were like swearing at God
or vandalizing the church,

that Breeds
were halfway to being redeemed
and praying extra hard
would open Heaven's gate.

They taught her

all boys had the devil's snake
and kissing on the keemootch   *on the sly or sneaky*
would put a bun in the oven,
land her in purgatory or hell
where she'd spend her days
fanning fires, picking lice
from the heads of demons.

By sixteen

they taught her

being a good wife
was to take it
on the chin, in the eye
or gut
even if the bun was half-baked.

The first baby
left blood in her panties,
an ache in her stomach,
then emptiness.

Father said
it was meant to be,
that forgiveness
was God's own teaching.

The other babies, well—
she didn't say.
That's another story.

I've Been Told

Halfbreed Heaven must be
handmade flowers of tissue,
poplar trees
forever in bloom,

the North and South Saskatchewan rivers
swirling and meeting
like the skirts, the hands
of cloggers
shuffling their moccasined feet.

I've been told

Halfbreed Heaven must be
old Gabriel at the gate
calling, "Tawow! Tawow!"   *Come in, you are welcome!*
toasting new arrivals, pointing
deportees
to the buffalo jump
or down the Great Canadian Railroad,
like Selkirk or MacDonald.

I've been told

Halfbreed Heaven must be
scuffed floors and furniture
pushed to one side,
grannies giggling in the kitchen,
their embroidered hankies
teasing and nudging
the sweetest sweet sixteen,
who will snare the eye
of the best jigger.

I've been told

Halfbreed Heaven must be
a wedding party
stretched to the new year,
into a wake, a funeral
then another wedding,
an endless brigade of happy faces
in squeaky-wheeled carts
loaded with accordions, guitars
and fiddles.

I've been told
Halfbreed Heaven must be
a rest-over for the Greats:
Hank Williams, Kitty Wells,
The Carter Family
and Hank Snow.

It must be
because I've been told so,

because I know
two Metis women who sing
beyond the blue.

Ode to the Greats (Northern Tribute)

Live

from the Grand Ole Opry
Hank cooed in all his glory

sailed

blue notes, fiddle strings
over airwaves,
pining lonesome,
his cheating heart
bursting through the voice box

up north

long before me, paved roads
and flushing toilets,

long before
the blues were reinvented,
sung
in a dozen shades of grey,
pale in comparison,
those rockabilly crooners
changed the soul
of heartland music

up north
before electric heat

they cuddled up to the woodstove,
toes tapping
along with Kitty, quivering

old-time twang,
her honky-tonk angels
bush and backroads
as Tennessee could never be,

crying blue
as Amigo's guitar
longing sweetly, strumming fingers
long past sundown

up north

a damn sight wild,
their generation,
half crazy on home brew
tuning hand-me-down guitars,
feet stomping
and lifting higher,
breaking into jigs
sweeping plywood floors

up north

long before power lines, oil rigs
burping underground

Patsy's syrup voice and sweet dreams
flowed from maple trees,
echoed far and wide
loons on the lake
crooning stars, pulling the moon

down
and through the voice box

Sara, A.P.
and Maybelle
picked autoharp strings,
chimed Clinch Mountain bluegrass
lonely
as muskeg reeds, spring frogs
pitching into chorus,
pining blue sky
orange, purple
crimson

up north

when the wind picks up,
blows sweet juniper
through the tent flaps,
the only thing to do
is sing, sing

strum and sing,
the northern lights
bright as Opryland,

dancing

the whole night through
they sang, their generation
sang
low and mean,

the poor man's blues,
richer than most

up north, before me,
before all roads
led down south

there was Heartland, USA

tuned in and

live

on the voice box
Jimmie and Wilf, all of
the Greats
chiming their Opry hi-dee-ho,
calling all lonesome rangers
to gather round
the voice box

up north

they sang and played
long after
the lights went down,

long after
the stage went silent,

the Greats
immortalized on records

that over time
skipped and scratched,

lifted me off to sleep

down south

my Greats, those two
homesick rounders
spoke of the north,
the glory days
as if it were only yesterday,
as if
one small ocean
could ever claim

their spirits, untamed,
sharp and tuned
as Hank's guitar.

SINGING HOME THE BONES

Prayer Song for the Returning of Names and Sons

YA-HEY-YA-HO
YA-HEY-YA-HEY
YA-HEYA
YA-HEY-HEY-YO

HIYA-HEY
HEY-HI-YA-HEY
YA-HEYA
YA-HEY-HEY-YO

HIYA-HEY
YA-HEY-YA-HEYA
YA-HEY-HEY-YO

HEY-HI-YA-HEY
HEY-HI-YA-HO

—prayer song taught to me by my adopted brother
Dale Awasis from Thunderchild First Nation,
Saskatchewan

â-haw, ni-châpanak Charlotte, *an invocation, my ancestral grandmothers*
Sarah, Mary ekwa Christiana.

â -haw,

kayâs ochi nikâwîmahk *my mothers of long ago*

natohta *listen*
my song, nikamowin *the song*

âw,
this song I am singing

to give you back the
polished swan bones,

the sewing awl, the birchbark bundle
holding the whetstone,

the drawing stone, the pounding
chokecherry stone, âw

the spirit of your iskwew   *woman*
names, the ones

not birthed from the belly
of their ships, not taken

from their manitowimasinahikan,   *bible*
âw, their great naming book

ni-châpanak Charlotte,   *my ancestral grandmothers*
Sarah, Mary

ekwa Christ-i-ana,   *and*
these are the names

I've thrown back across the water,
I've given back

to their God
who has two hearts, two tongues

to speak with.
âw, natohta   *listen*

96

my song, nikamowin   *the song*
the renaming song

I am singing
five generations later,

natohta   *listen*
my prayer song

so you will be called,
sung as:

Tattooed From The Lip To The Chin Woman,
êy-hey! Sung as:

She Paints Her Face With Red Ochre,
êy-hey! Sung as:

Charm Woman Who Is Good To Make A Nation
Woman, êy-hey!

I give you back
ni-châpanak

the names to name
the names of bones, oskana   *the bones*

you laid down
to build them a house, âw

the blood, mihko   *blood*
and warm skin

earth, askîy   *earth*
that built them an empire.

natohta   *listen*
my song, nikamowin   *the song*

the prayer song
I am singing

to bring back
your stolen sons

whose sons and sons
and their missing bones

are unsung geese
lost in a country

across the water
ni-châpanak   *my ancestral grandmothers*

I've thrown back
your names;

nâmoya kîyawaw   *you are not*
Charlotte, Sarah, Mary

ekwa Christiana.   *and*
nâmoya kîyawaw môniyaskwewak.   *you are not white women*

â-haw, ni-châpanak   *an invocation, my ancestral grandmothers*
kayâs ochi nikâwîmahk   *my mothers of long ago*

natohta   *listen*

my song, nikamowin   *the song*

this prayer song
I am singing.

êy-hey!

Note: My châpanak of five generations past and my mothers of long ago came to find me while I was researching my maternal genealogy. The meticulous records that the Hudson's Bay Company kept on their employees, now available in their archives, serve as an invaluable source of information for many Metis and half-breed people, especially those who originate from western Canada. My grandfathers of that era, many of whom came from the Orkneys and London, arrived in Canada in the mid- to late 1700s. Some of them, such as James Peter Whitford, landed at York Factory, one of the Company's principal posts. Records state his full name, the parish he belonged to in London, the date he entered service, his various appointments and positions, the dates of his postings and his death on May 5, 1818 at Red River Settlement. Below this information, it simply states: *Wife: Sarah, an Indian woman. Married pre-1795 at Severn(?) Buried 27 Apr. 1845, 70 years old, at Upper Church.* I am certain my châpan Sarah, my kayâs ochi nikâwî—who eventually gave birth to eight children—came to my ancestor/ grandfather carrying a name too sacred for him to pronounce. During my research I began to talk to her in a language that caused her bones to shift beneath the earth. I asked her to help me, her little ni-châpanis, to find and sing the proper names, even though the old names are forever lost. The women of my blood, my other châpanak, came to listen. I was grateful to have made this connection, to be a part of a ceremony that cannot be recorded.

Women Who Forgot the Taste of Limes
Letter to ni-châpan Mary

ni-châpan, if I take ki-cihcânikan, *my ancestor, your fingerbone*
press it to their lips,
will they remember the taste of limes,
sea-salt bled into their grandfathers' skin?

If I pull from this bag of rattling bones
the fiddle, the bow bone,
if I go down to the lazy Red,
lay singing in the grass

will the faces of our ancestors
take shape in clouds
and will the clouds name themselves,
each river-lot stolen?

If I take ki-tôkanikan, ni-châpan, *your hipbone*
place on them a pack to bear
will they know the weight of furs,
kawâpahtamiwuk chî *will they see?*

the city is made of blood, wîni *bone marrow*
stains their grandmothers' aprons,
swims deep in the flesh, a grave of history,
a dry bone song.

ni-châpan, if I take ki-kiskatikan, *your shinbone*
will they offer up the streets,
lay open their doors and say I'm welcome?
Or if I take ki-tâpiskanikan, *your jawbone*

place it scolding on Portage and Main
will all the dead Indians
rise up from the cracks, spit bullets
that made silent our talk?

If I take ki-mâwikan, ni-châpan   *your backbone*
I could say to them
I'm not afraid of gunshots, stones
or the table I sit at—

this table where I drink tea with ghosts
who share my house and the words
to keep it clean.
ni-châpan, if I take ki-cihcânikan,   *my great-great grandmother,*
                                               your fingerbone

press it to their lips
will they remember the taste of limes,
hold silent their sour tongues
for once?

The Repatriation of Mrs. Ida M. Scofield

I. The Family Portrait: Portage la Prairie, Manitoba, c. 1904–1905

It is all here   unravelling
in black and white
the meaning of salvage, the last
sepia-toned remnant

of your gleaming white life,
the stiff likeness of yourself
appearing more the photographer's prop,
the settee

holding the seized woman
whose hair is neatly piled,
pinned into place   you waiting
to tear off the thick brocade dress

and throat pin, this presentation
of perfect ordinance
caught in tatters   fraying apart
all in good black order.

It is all here, Ida:
you, the portrait in the portrait.
Knotted and carefully stitched,
nothing visible, nothing misplaced

except for the soft-shaping bones
inside, my grandfather's
small body of exile, the bastard bones
of freedom   freedom

from the tit-tat talk of town,
the man to your right
who is raging beneath his collar,
who is not my blood—

my blood name
that is not my grandfather's name,
the name
given to our history.

And it is all here
in the eyes of the woman beside you,
grey and death-marching
her lips pocked with crucifixion

that I can see   in black and white
the meaning of salvage,
this careful unbolting
of your life's fabric,

although the drop behind you
is silk, such lovely silk
your eyes have cut past
the photographer's vision

already gone   away dear Ida,
from his composition.

Conversation with the Poet
Who didn't know my aunty

This story is told in oral tradition in a voice much older than mine, a voice whose thought process and first language is Cree. The story, though written in English, is a translation. I've heard old people speak in both Cree and English many times and I am immediately drawn into their rhythms, the poetry of their voices.

a few years ago   at a reading
of erotic poetry
a poet read a poem
by another poet
about a toothless Eskimo woman
in a bar
looking for someone, anyone
to buy her a drink   and
what she did, what
that Eskimo woman did for a drink

—

Long ago when my aunty was no longer Mean Man's wife—
Punching Bag Woman she was called—she had met a moniyâw, a
white man. He was the one who called her Good Cooking Day
Woman, or Good Laundry Day Woman, or sometimes, Good With
The Money Day Woman.

Now, my aunty had TB in her lungs—which took her from Edmonton
down to a hospital in Vancouver. I used to hear about it at that time; it
must have been hard for her.

She had three sons, my aunty did. But two of her boys got sick and
died in Wabasca. Her other boy, John Houle he was called, was killed
in a car accident coming home for Christmas. I used to hear
her talk about it sometimes. She'd say to me, *One night back home I
was sitting having tea and I looked out at the clothesline and sure enough*

there were three owls sitting there, just sitting there hooting away on my
clothesline. It's true, she told me. *And those owls, those owls started*
making somersaults, spinning around and around like this, she told me.

a few years ago   at a reading
of erotic poetry
a poet read a poem
by another poet
about a toothless Eskimo woman

who could be:

ni-châpan, Hunting To Feed The Family Woman   *my great-great-*
     grandmother

who could be:

ni-mâmâ, Holding Up The Walls Woman   *my mother*

who could be:

a kaskitewiyas-iskwew,   *a black woman*

sekipatwâw-iskwew,   *a Chinese woman*

moniyâw-iskwew   *a white woman*

running from a white man,
any man
into the arms of a poet

in a bar
looking for someone, anyone
to buy her a drink

—

My aunty, as I was saying here before, lost her boys early on.
That is how I came to be her son: "nikosis, now you take the place
of my John," she used to say. And I treated her as my mother:
ni-mâmâsis, my little mother, I used to call her. My own mother
—Dorothy was her name—did not mind this arrangement, for
it was good for me to have two mothers.

It was these women who raised me by themselves. They were poor,
my mothers, but it did not seem to matter—there were many
things to keep a young boy occupied: books, music, stories and
beadwork. I recall one time watching my aunty sew some moccasins.
So interested was I that I kept moving closer and closer to
her work. She did not seem to mind this . . . Now, my little mother
used to sew with very long threads and her needle would move
very quickly. But this time I did not pay attention, so engrossed
with the moccasins was I. She must have known this, for she took
her sâponikan, that needle, and poked me right on the nose. *awas,
ma-kôt!* she said. *Go on, big nose!* That is what she told me.

—

a few years ago   at a reading
of erotic poetry
a poet read a poem
by another poet
about a toothless Eskimo woman

she was fat, a seal
for the taking

she was dirty, a bag
of muskox bones
crawling with lice

she was dumb, her language
click, click
made people laugh

she was looking
for someone, anyone
to buy her a drink

—

I will not say my mothers did not have trouble with drinking or
they did not lose days keeping the house in order. It is true: they
had weaknesses here and there, just like other people.

And as far as my little mother goes, though she loved me a great
deal, she did not get over losing her boys. I guess that is why today
I speak so proudly of her, for she taught me many good things.

—

a few years ago   at a reading
of erotic poetry
a poet read a poem
by another poet
about a toothless Eskimo woman

and what she did   that woman
did for a drink.

It was in a bar:

it could be
the one from my childhood,

a room of white faces, a poetry hall
of uproarious mouths,

a room of unbound limbs
laughing
deep in their bones

or it could be
my aunty's rape bed, the man
who took her like a monument,
step after violent step

or it could be
her deathbed, all sixty-nine years
of her
lost in the translation
of a policeman's report

it could be, yes
the bed
where she, told me stories

â-ha, the bed
where I laid dreaming

—

This is as much as I am able to tell about my aunty. But there is another thing, one more thing you should know: I loved her very much and I still think of her whenever I am lonesome. ekosi, I am done.

Conversation with My Stepfather

Now that I've bundled my mother's bones,
Sang them home

On the backs of four aging horses,
I can tell you, old man,

It'll take more than the wrecking ball
Of your fist, the hoe of your heel

To rattle this house, undo
The frame of my timbers

That held up each death-marching year
You'd buried me over

And over in the yard
Or the pedophile down the street

You'd prayed to do you some kindness,
Some small, traceless bone act.

But here, see old man,
I've laid out my mother's bundle;

Put your eyes upon her jawbone
What voice will you give it?

Put your eyes upon her cheekbone
What prayer will you speak it?

Put your eyes upon her collarbone
What song will you sing it?

Put your eyes upon her wristbone
What offering will you bring it?

Put your eyes upon her shinbone
What root will you heal it?

Put your eyes upon her backbone
What bag of shame

What medicine bag of words
Will you give her?

Old man, because of you
I've travelled four lives

On the backs
Of four aging horses. But see

Now I am painted
And I've built my house

From the last of your marrow,
From the last of your bones.

The Dancer (Club Mix)

see him   he is
un touchable, unreadable,

more lovely than smooth gravity
glistening

down the length of his body,
his small hips, his tight

perfect ass swinging
up to the platform, all motion

swivelling on his golden ball-bearings.
see him   moving

on rhythmic cue, he is
beautiful, so unreadable

the curve of his spine
is the jigsaw puzzle

we want to put together, the
damp lush scene   he is

getting paid
to unlock his vaulted package,

the overflowing box
of our stone-dragging youth.

but   we are falling at
his feet, longing

to take each biblical toe
into our mouths, praying

to be his stigmata, oh
his incubus-tongued angel,

love-eyed, all sugar-eyed
like the e-queens bopping high,

messed on their own love trip tripping
though we're all chasing

locks, zippers,
the elastic band

holding his jockstrap together.
but   he is

getting paid a doctor's wage
to be that fat man's murderer,

the old troll's executioner, a killer
made more lovely

stroking the blade of his
oh so deadly nipples.

and beneath the red light he
will be the boy in school

who beat the shit out of us for
looking; he will be

our velvet fuck, our burly-man prince,
our mint-

flavoured lamb, our saviour . . . but see
he is grazing down his belly,

all ten fingers
an arsenal to keep us smouldering.

we can smell
the gun powder between his legs

and we want to pop, pop,
pop

because he is getting paid
to fuck our minds, getting paid

to make us forget our mirrors,
the crystal-dropping twinks

floating to the dance floor,
bouncing like Muppets.
because   he is
getting paid

to make the drag queens feel
like real women, getting paid

to be their spank-spank boy,
the roughneck quarterback

running them past the goal line
of snickering small towns,

fathers who just wouldn't understand.
but see   he is

all muscle, his perfect ass swinging.
he is our golden trumpet,

our rainbow flag anthem:
Everybody wants to be somebody

Everybody wants to be somebody
Everybody wants to be somebody

Everybody wants to be somebody

and he is   getting paid
by the man upstairs who

discovered his ass,
knew it

would be a money-maker, a ching-
ching factory of coke-den lies,

a bar tab of heart
heart

heartbreak—but see   he is
un touchable, unreadable,

more lovely than smooth gravity
glistening, sliding

down the length of his

       bones.

but he is getting paid
at the end of the night and

these are some of the bones
he takes home; his

mother's narrow foot
dancing away from him, his

grandmother's hairpins
falling into a drawer

deep in his memory, the blood
bursting inside his aunty's head

while she was sleeping,
drunk . . . and his own

aching bones,
half-breed and kicking.

yet later, swallowed by
the empty mouths of our beds,

we will think of him.
we will make him pay.

he will be our second-hand   doll
and we will use him

for free, as if
he meant nothing.

I Don't Know My Body Without You

Little wonder
I don't know my body
without all ten fingers of you

when you ask
if I've touched myself,
an ocean between us, here

on this island torn naked by rain,
fondled by days of rain,
a spectacle of never-ending guilt

like the church across the street,
its voyeuristic steeple
rising and rising

as if in this moment of hesitation
I'm certain to hear the bells,
the chiming

of your faraway bones, although
really what I want
is for you to come, come singing

and I want
to be your pulpit, your hymn book,
the steam organ

you've come to play. Little wonder
I don't know my body
without your tongue,

that unruly boy
disturbing the choir. But then you ask
from the confessional of our bed

if I've touched myself, if
I think of praying
to another god, as if I would.

            Little wonder
I don't know my body,
the scripture, the illegible parchment

of my own skin
without your eyes,
those two winged demons,

hazel as hell. And you ask
as if declaring the apocalypse,
if I've touched myself

            and all I can say is
I want you to come,
come singing.

and I want, sweet angel,
to finally come
home.

Invocation for the Bones in My Back

So you haven't broken yet   bones
thirty-nine years I've carried my
mother's hungry baby, my father's
throwaway chromosomes   and bones

I will sing the song
ni-châpan sang to all her children,   *my great-great grandmother*
sing you good bones

the bannock, the partridge song
holding upright my vertebrae,
the long-ago weight

of my stepfather's fists,
those soldiers
keeping watch down my spine,

oh spine, how can I praise—
sing you the hate-filled packs
I've buckled under,

the loads of loss, the bags
carrying my mother's fear,
my aunty's dead children,

my grandmother's finger
pointing to God   and goddamn
the cracks, the splintered

bones I've moved from house to house

unpacking you, spine, and
I've never once given you thought,

a song for the men
whose balls I've broken, a chorus
as simple as doe-rae-me

for the tra-la-la
of my oh-so-stubborn bones,
for the poems

I've sucked from the marrow,
for the thinness of my generosity,
the bundles

I've allowed to be opened, the ones
I've burned and cried over
the weight of unflinching ashes.
so you haven't broken yet   bones
thirty-nine years I've carried
my mother's hungry baby, my father's
throwaway chromosomes
and I'm no worse
than the jeweller's son

whose pawnshop bones
have sold their singing.

NEW POEMS

The Dissertation

The poet in him is an assassin,
a killer, cantankerous and absolute.
He suffers the end
as do all great martyrs.
To call her a stalker is overkill.
He was her selection. No fuss.
No dazzle.

She overtook his poetry like a landlord,
rented him a room in his life
where she could study his polemic
or lack thereof.
At first it was flattering like a hat or shoes,
a coexistence of sorts.
A treaty. A shadow.

But then arrived the microscope
and she set to work, the academic,
prodding and jotting,
jotting and prodding.
She even annexed his speech,
the Indian words she was so drawn to.
It gave her own language authenticity,

a ring of wild metaphor.
It was ballsy, even magical
how she slipped into his skin,
the poet, who in the end
she surmised was beyond saving.
To call her a stalker is overkill.
He was simply her selection.

No fuss. No dazzle.
She suffers her life's work
as does any great scholar.

astâm pî-miciso
(Come, eat!)

I am all laid out on the table
that has seen birth and death.

astâm pî-miciso   *Come, eat!*
while I am hot and steaming.

Hah, take first my fingers,
all ten of them,

a basket that holds
the plumpest of berries. iya,   *exclamation of great pleasure*

make sweet your tongue
that'll give way to humming.

I am all laid out on the table,
a wooden bowl of boiled bones.

astâm pî-miciso.   *Come, eat!*
I am begging to be greased,

held to your mouth for sucking.
Hah, behold the table

that has seen birth and death,
this abundance

where I give you my fattest parts
to be chewed like Wihtikiw.   *Cannibal, Legendary Eater of Humans*

awiyâ! Make sharp your teeth   *slang for "ouch, it hurts!"*
where I am most tender.

126

Then there is the tray
made of spruce and bark.

It is oval and holds perfectly
the jackfish of my belly, hah,

the wild onions.
I say, astâm pî-miciso   *Come, eat!*

while I am spread out,
set upon this table

that has seen birth and death.
Here, too, is a duck

whose breast is my tongue
having nested all summer.

Now make it fly up, call it
to where you are warmest.

iya, sing it to the place   *exclamation of great pleasure*
you are saving for ceremony.

pî-miciso! pî-miciso!   *Eat, eat!*
I am your soup pot,

a prayer-sung stew.
My legs are two rabbits

and these are my toes
to be bitten like turnips. iya

I am all laid out
for you to see, to taste

the feast of me. â-ha,   *Yes*
look to the left

where I am a small bowl
of dry meat.

Hold me between your lips
and eat me slowly,

scared little bites.
Then I will say to you,

kî-kîspohn? The dead will see   *Are you full, satisfied?*
what we've done and

the living will go away
with crumbs in their mouths.

Then the drums will pulse
thu-thump, thu-thump

and you will be all motion, a shadow
like the dogs outside.

The Ship

He is building a ship
With his eyes, the bistro-boy
Is building a ship
With his eyes.

He is building a ship
So soundly
I want to give him my mouth,
My youth

That crawls the deck of his lashes,
My tongue
Because young Jonah
Is building a ship

With his eyes, the bistro-boy
Is building a ship
With his eyes.
Jonah is small

And not my type.
He rides the bus.
He drives a skateboard.
But the winter light

Is a hot-lipped whore
Falling across his lashes,
Who is dangerous after seven
Because it's in this light

He uses his eyes to cut pie,
His curls to make
The salt & pepper shakers
Come.

I come each day
To see the progress.
I come to watch
The compass of his fingers.

Because I am tortuous
Jonah does not know
At closing
I think about the heat
People leave in chairs
And how if the chairs
Were his legs
I would arrange them a part.

I would make him wide.
I would throw him open.
I would make him take on water
Because he is building

A vessel, a ship
With his eyes.
But he is not in love,
The bistro-boy

Is not in love.
He is merely a body of newness.
I can smell his salt,
I can taste him.

Jonah does not know
When I draw my evening bath
I am only nine floors
Above him.

Beneath my clothes
My bones are near useless.
I am as good as land-locked.
Two provinces away

My captain keeps our ship afloat.
Because of this
I drink lattes alone.
I keep quiet like a foghorn.

But from my chair
I watch the chairs and I watch
Jonah, the bistro-boy
Building his ship.

Day in, day out
I am more in love
Because he is tireless, a sea of fingers
So perfectly thorough.

My Man Loves a Fisherman

My man will tell you
I love him like a fisherman,

all hooks when I am easy,
a far-flung net

when I am trolling,
crawling the blackest bottom.

My man will tell you—
because it's true—

I am my own worst navigator.
I troll in places long depleted,

hoping the dead
will offer up their apologies.

Like me, they, too, were fishermen,
a bunch of anchor-hearted bitches

too stubborn to move along.
Yet I love them like Noah

because they were organized in their boats.
They refused the flood, flat out.

So this is how I came to be a fisherman,
a doctor-of-the-depths.

This also means I am water savvy
And I can smell bad weather.

Either way, my man will tell you
I love him like a fisherman.

Sometimes I think he's useless at sea.
But he's a master with knots

and fishing things like cutting nets.
He has a good sense of direction,

my butcher, who didn't sign up for this.
He will tell you
I love him like a fisherman
because I do. I love him

the way Noah loved the animals.
In him I see land,

a place to take momentary rest.
My man will tell you

I am more than scales and eyes,
even when I can't see it.

The Dark

for Neal

We are a fort of bones,
you and I
marching toward sleep,

each of us
holding our broken things
like defiant boys; for you

the stiff lip of your father,
for me
the stray dog of mine.

We are a stronghold of bolts
and steel. We are fortified,
two bastions of stone

that you and I
in our private dark
build with such precision

there is no time for sleep,
there is no time
for trifling or cursing the clock.

There is only the time
between shadows and daybreak
we can be watchful, safe

as sixty stone men.
We are a fort of bones
marching toward sleep.

We are a fort of bones
where you shelter your woman,
where I, the doorman,

lay out my ring of keys,
unlocking my lover
one by one. I give to him

what you give to her;
the sleepy eye, poems
that grow from all the cracks.
Still we hitchhike into the wrong dreams.
We are monsters here with nowhere
to house our bruises.

We are casualties without our stones,
our bolts and steel.
We are twigs set out for dancing.

Maybe it is simple,
we are nerves turned inside out.
Maybe we are holy men at work.

But we are a fort of bones
you and I.
We march toward sleep

like two quaking boys,
each of us
a resurrection in the dark.

My Husband Goes to War

My husband goes to war
Wearing little more than accusation,
The bag I bought him
He has stuffed with green bullets,
The map
Leading back to me, his territory.

My husband goes to war.
We did not have relations the night before
To keep his vigour,
To keep him gunning for the Cree
Who crawled into bed with us.
My husband goes to war.

My husband goes to war
With sculpting wax in his hair.
He will scalp the Cree
Just to be political. He will
Hang the proof on his Armani belt.
My husband goes to war.

My husband does not like the Cree.
He is young with ideas, a filmmaker.
He is crafty, pretty
And sure-footed. He is on the kîmoc   *sly or sneaky*
In a haughty sort of way.
He is a Virgo.

My husband is a Virgo.
My husband goes to war.
My husband goes to war.
He will storm Winnipeg Beach.

He will kill the Cree.
He will cut his balls off.

He will drop them in the soup pot,
He will eat them.
My husband goes to war.
We did not have relations
The night before
To keep his vigour, to keep him

Gunning for the Cree.
My husband goes to war.
My husband worries I love the Cree.
He worries I'll leave
For chokecherries and fat.
He worries I am hungry for wild-wîyas.   *meat*

My husband goes to war
Wearing little more than accusation,
The bag I bought him
He has stuffed with green bullets.
My husband goes to war.
I am his territory, his discovery.

The Man Who Forgot to Claim His Son

Babi, the day   *grandmother*
I am most angry at my father

my lover
finds a dreidle in the yard,   *a spinning top used at Chanukah*

A brokhe he tells me   *a blessing*
small and silent

as sure as I am the son
of the man

who forgot to claim me.
Babi,

it has been made kaddosh   *holy or sacred*
by the fingers of a child.

And Babi,
it has come the day

I am most angry at my father.
A sign, a brokhe   *a blessing*

my lover tells me
I must keep looking

through this rag-bag
of my father's suits, the pockets

of his lies.
Oy, his not-so-holy stories.

And Babi,
tonight when the ghosts of old men

button their coats
in the north end of Winnipeg,

here in our warm house
where things are lost

and found
I will make latkes
and we will eat applesauce
until I am sweet again.

Babi, the day
I am most angry at my father

my lover finds
a dreidle in the yard.

When he is sleeping
I will place this sign

upon the table.
I will light two candles,

one for me, my father.
I will touch it to my lips,

kiss kaddosh   *holy or sacred*
each Hebrew letter.

Tonight Babi,
all is as should be,

all is well here,
here

a miracle has happened.

I'll Teach You Cree

with the tip of my spring tongue, ayîki   *frog*
your mouth will be the web
catching apihkêsis words,   *spider*
a crawling-out ceremony
that cannot be translated.

hâw, pîkiskwê!   *Now, speak!*

I'll teach you Cree, nêhiyawêwin   *the Cree language*
that is the taste
of pimiy êkwa saskatômina   *fat and saskatoon berries*
Your mouth with be the branches
I am picking clean,
a summer heat ceremony
that cannot be translated.

hâw, pîkiskwê!   *Now, speak!*

I'll teach you Cree
in the winter, pipon   *winter*
when the dogs curl against our backs.
Your mouth will be pawâcakinâsis-pîsim   *the frost exploding moon*
that cannot be translated.
It will be a ceremony.

hâw, pîkiskwê!   *Now, speak!*

I'll teach you Cree
ê-kohk mistahi ê-sâkihitan.   *because I love you a lot*
It will be in the fall, this ceremony.
You will have the mouth of a beaver,
thick and luminescent.

I will make my camp there
ê-kohk mistahi ê-sâkihitan.   *because I love you a lot*
This cannot be translated.

hâw, pîkiskwê!   *Now, speak!*

This Is My Blanket

"An Indian and his blanket were inseparable."
—Barry Friedman, *Country Home Magazine*
(October, 2008)

I am nothing without my blanket.
This is the key to the storehouse.
I am in charge here.

This is my blanket,
spectacularly hued, wildly patterned.
An end to the Indian wars.

I am federally licensed to write this poem.
I am nothing without my blanket.
This is the big aha of the whole thing.

This is the key to the storehouse,
brimming with treasure.
Hail the missing and murdered,

the names yet recorded. I am in charge here.
It's not that I am a country wife to be swooned.
It's not that straightforward.

I wear this blanket to keep my mother warm.
She lived in a meat truck
made homey with doilies and rag-rugs.

Each month she cashed her cheque
because she was federally licensed to.
This is the big aha of the whole thing.

She was nothing without her blanket,
my mama, the Perpetual Lady of Sorrows.
But this is not to say

she was easily swooned.
She wore her blanket like perfume.
It was her formal dress, a real zinger.

I am nothing without my blanket.
This is the key to my aunty's house.
She got raped here.
On this blanket
spectacularly hued, wildly patterned.
An end to the Indian wars.

The man who did it
was federally licensed.
Now her blanket is a living, breathing textile,

not something you fish out of the closet
when it starts snowing.
This is the big aha of the whole thing.

This is my blanket.
This is the key to the storehouse.
I am in charge here.